Cursive Penmanship Workbook for Kids

Introduction to a Modern Script Font with Easy Step by Step
Instructions for Kids

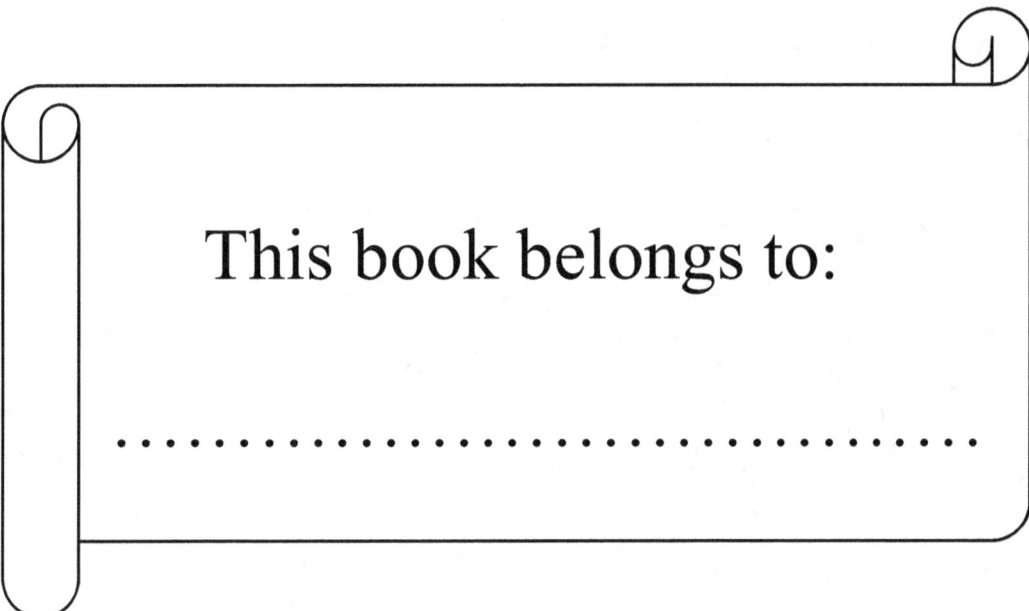

This book belongs to:

....

Not Your Typical Cursive Handwriting Workbook!

Cursive penmanship has become a lost artform. However, this workbook tries to revive that artform and combine the standard cursive style with modern calligraphy.

As we stated in many of our other handwriting workbooks before, cursive handwriting has various benefits which also bear with them some solid scientific backup. Some of the most important are:

1. Fine development of motor skills.

2. Reinforced learning abilities.

3. Improved spelling skills.

This book, however, was not designed to teach standard cursive handwriting, but something much grander. That's why it would be advantageous if your child would already know how to write in the standard form of cursive. (If not, we have some great books designed to teach that too!)

To keep it as simple and enjoyable as possible, we kept our usual format designed for kids:

Part I – Contains worksheets for each letter of the alphabet (with step by step instructions).

Part II – Contains worksheets for complete words.

So, what is this workbook really about? Essentially, it's an introduction to a handwriting style with calligraphic elements. This workbook builds up on the traditional handwriting style and allows your child to discover an easy way of adding a nuanced touch of calligraphy to his or her handwriting.

In addition, we added a table with a comparison between the *Standard Cursive Style* and the *Modern Script Font* taught in this workbook.

Standard Cursive	*Modern Script Font*
A a	*A a*
B b	*B b*
C c	*C c*
D d	*D d*
E e	*E e*
F f	*F f*
G g	*G g*

H h	H h
I i	I i
J j	J j
K k	K k
L l	L l
M m	M m
N n	N n
O o	O o

$P\ p$		$P\ p$	
$Q\ q$		$Q\ q$	
$R\ r$		$R\ r$	
$S\ s$		$S\ s$	
$T\ t$		$T\ t$	
$U\ u$		$U\ u$	
$V\ v$		$V\ v$	
$W\ w$		$W\ w$	

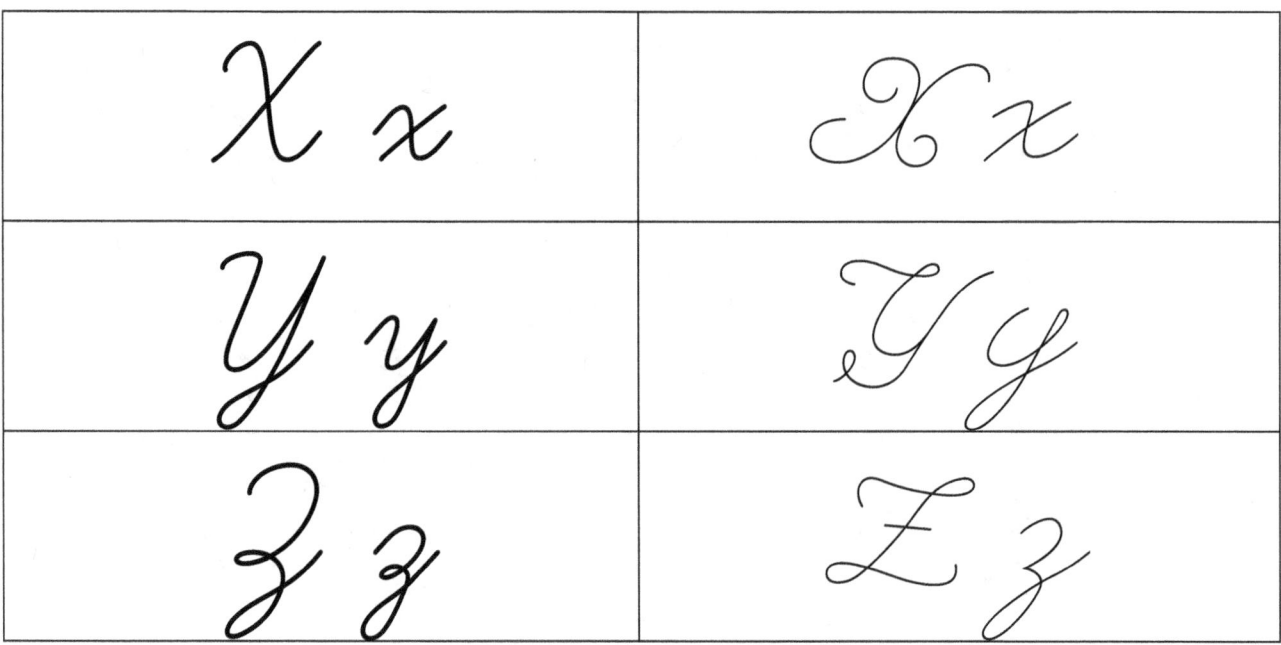

Over time, your child can allow this modern script font to evolve naturally and developed into something unique to his or her personality.

Tips for a Memorable Learning Experience

This modern script font is obviously a bit more difficult to master than the standard cursive style. That's why we also included some tips for beginners. These are not mandatory but could prove useful and turn the entire learning experience into something much more enjoyable:

1. Start with the right equipment

    As mentioned before, this style is a mix between standard handwriting and modern calligraphy. That's why any writing utensil could be used. However, even if they are a bit tricky to master at first, pointed dib nips present obvious advantages when it comes to this style of writing. The pointed sharp nibs allow swirling flourishes and thin strokes to come much more easily.

2. Prepare the workspace

    First, you should clear the table and prepare a clean and organized practice environment.

    Second, you should prepare the supplies: a pen with a pointed dib nip (if you decided to use one), ink, workbook, and additional paper.

3. Lead by example

    A calligraphy pen might be difficult to hold at first, especially for a child. That's why you should show your kid how to properly hold the pen. Discuss and see what feels most comfortable.

    Go over each letter from the previous table in order to offer a clear vision on how the modern script font differs from the standard handwriting style.

4. Have fun

In addition to completing the exercises in this book. It might be useful to allow your child to scribble and draw first on an additional piece of paper. This will make the calligraphy pen feel more comfortable and could take any pressure off the child.

Remember that in order for such a style of handwriting to develop easily and evolve naturally, the entire practice must occur with ease and fun. The art of penmanship is something that can offer a unique touch to any written content. The learning experience should, therefore, be done with love so that the same feeling can be seen on paper.

That being said. Let's begin with **Part I** of our workbook.

Letter A

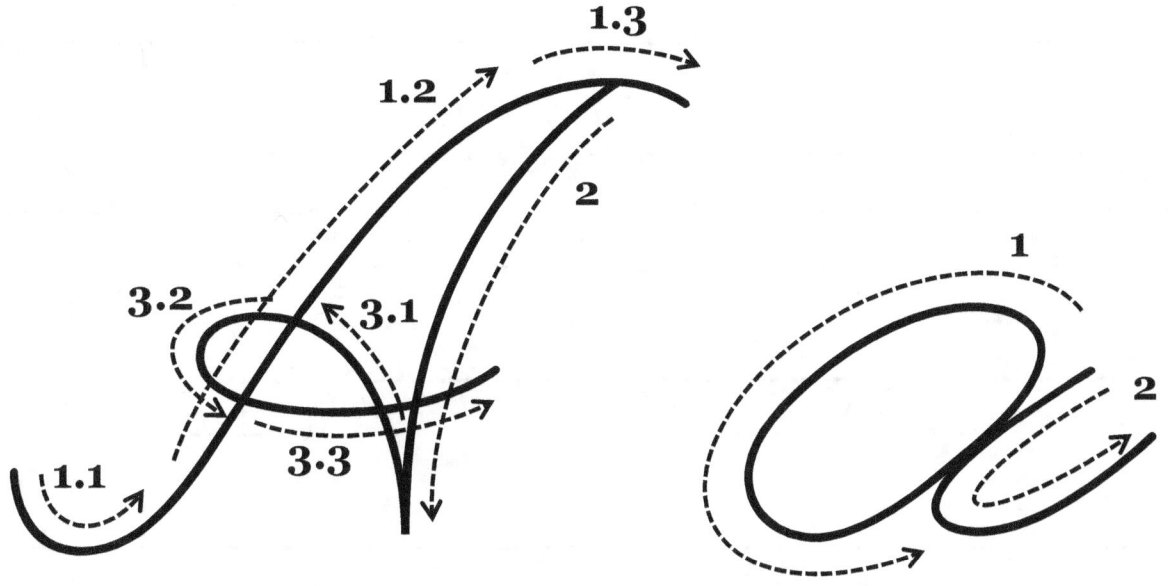

A A A A A A A A

A A A

A

A

A

A

A

A

A

A

a *a*

13

Letter B

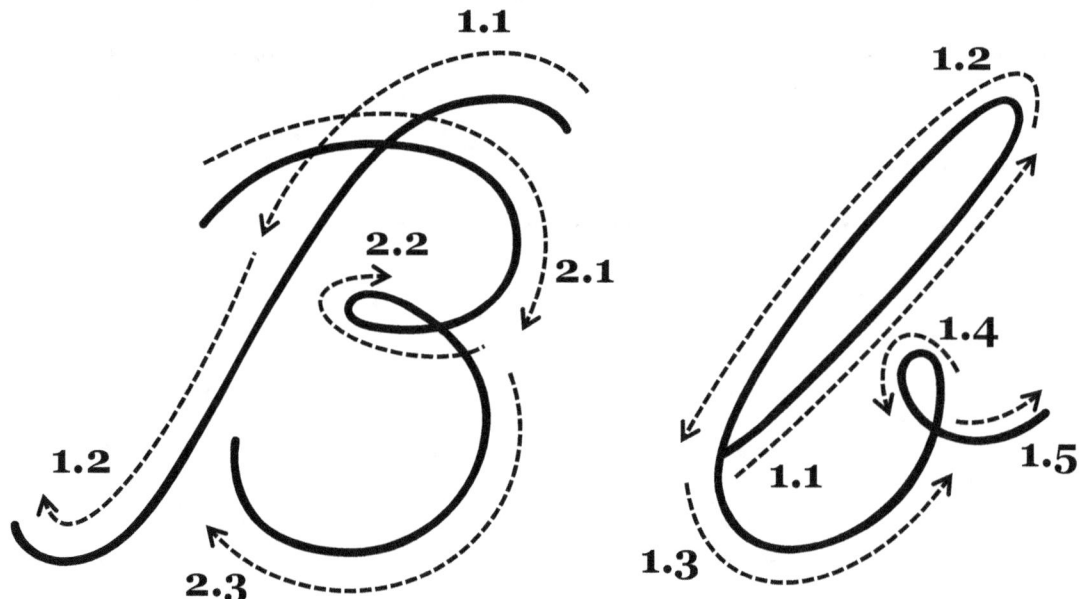

$\mathcal{B}\ \mathcal{B}\quad \mathcal{B}\quad \mathcal{B}\quad \mathcal{B}\quad \mathcal{B}\quad \mathcal{B}$

b *b* *b* *b* *b* *b* *b* *b* *b* *b*

b *b* *b*

b

b

b

b

b

b

b

Letter C

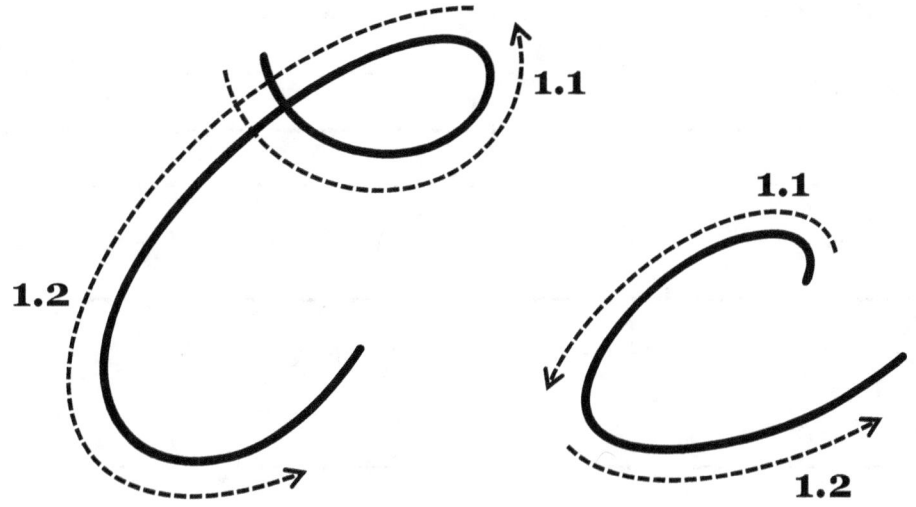

C C C C C C C C C C

C C C

C

C

C

C

C

C

C

C

Letter D

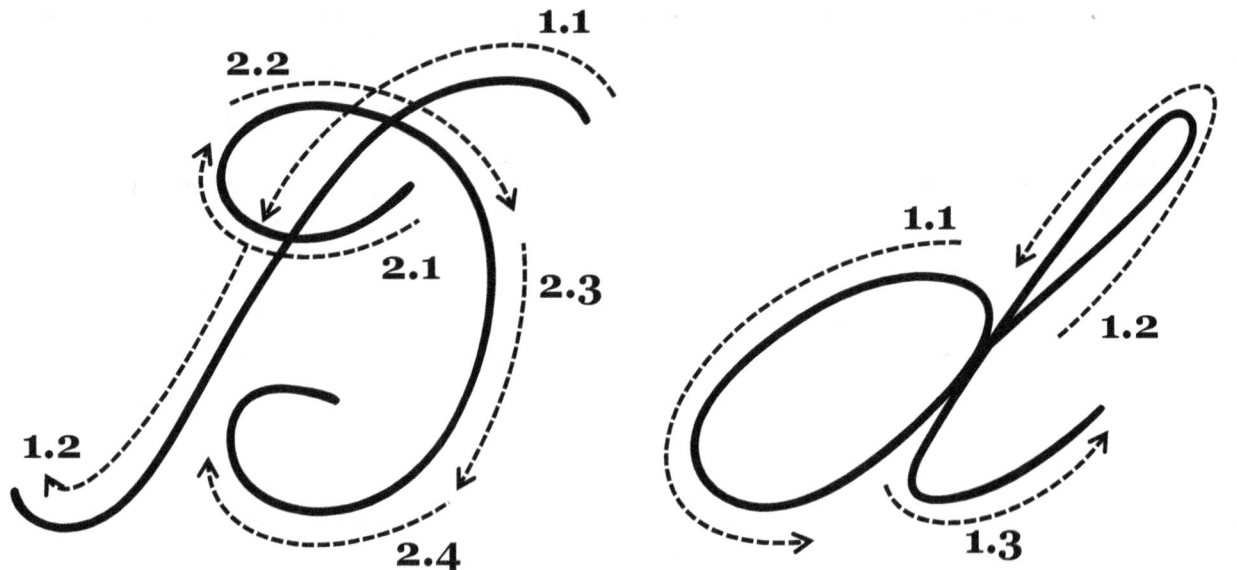

d d d d d d d

d d d

d

d

d

d

d

d

d

Letter E

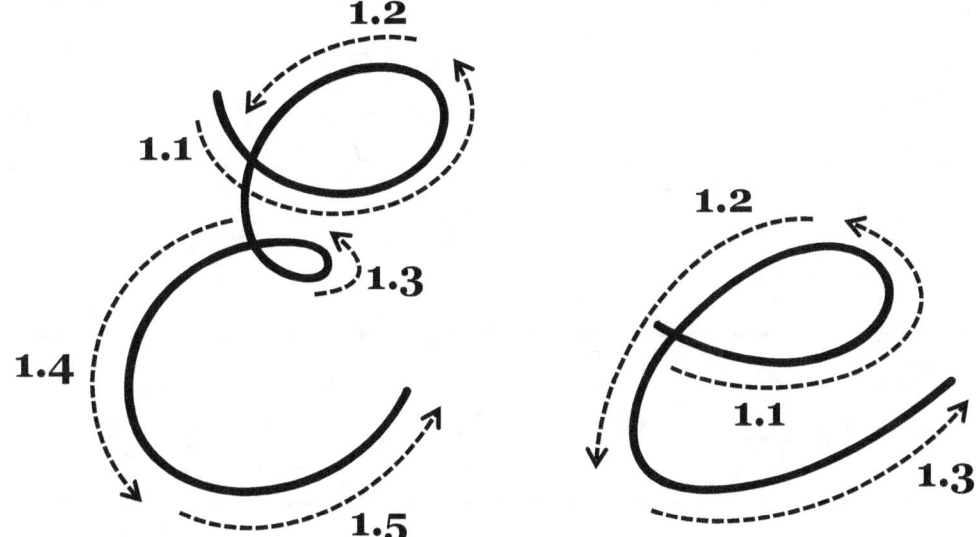

e e e e e e e e e

Letter F

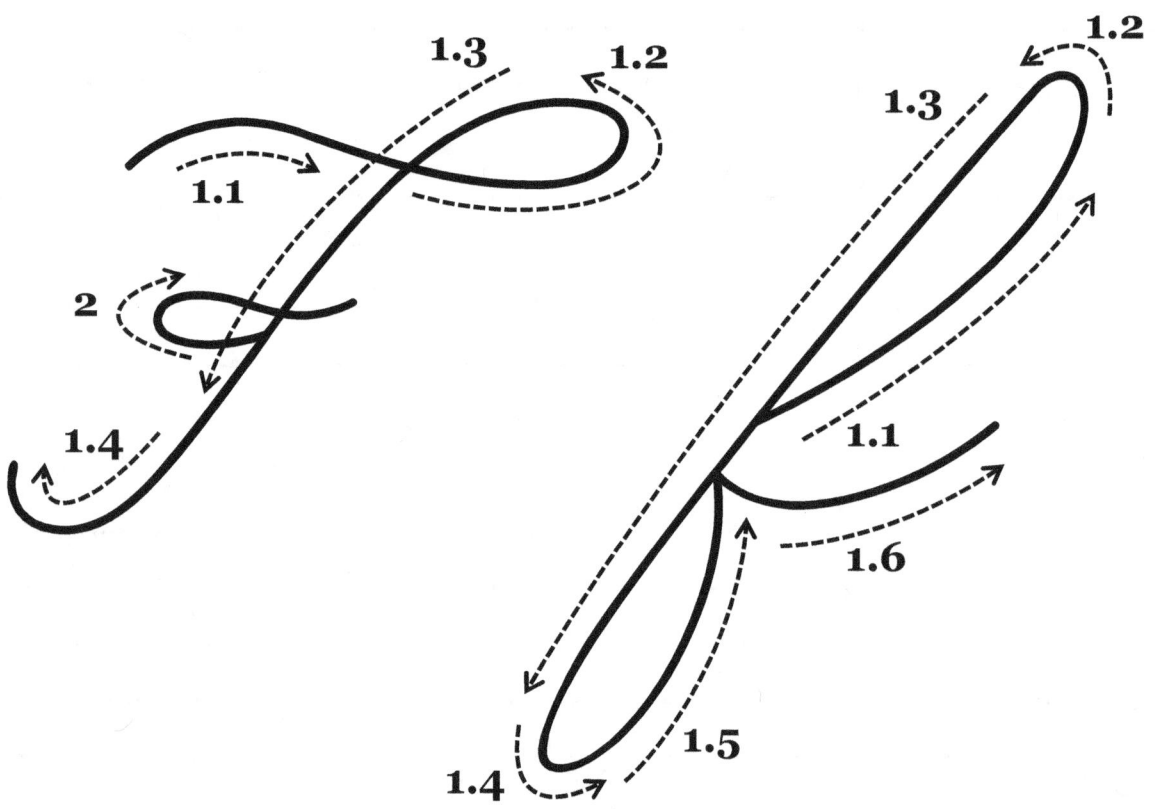

Letter G

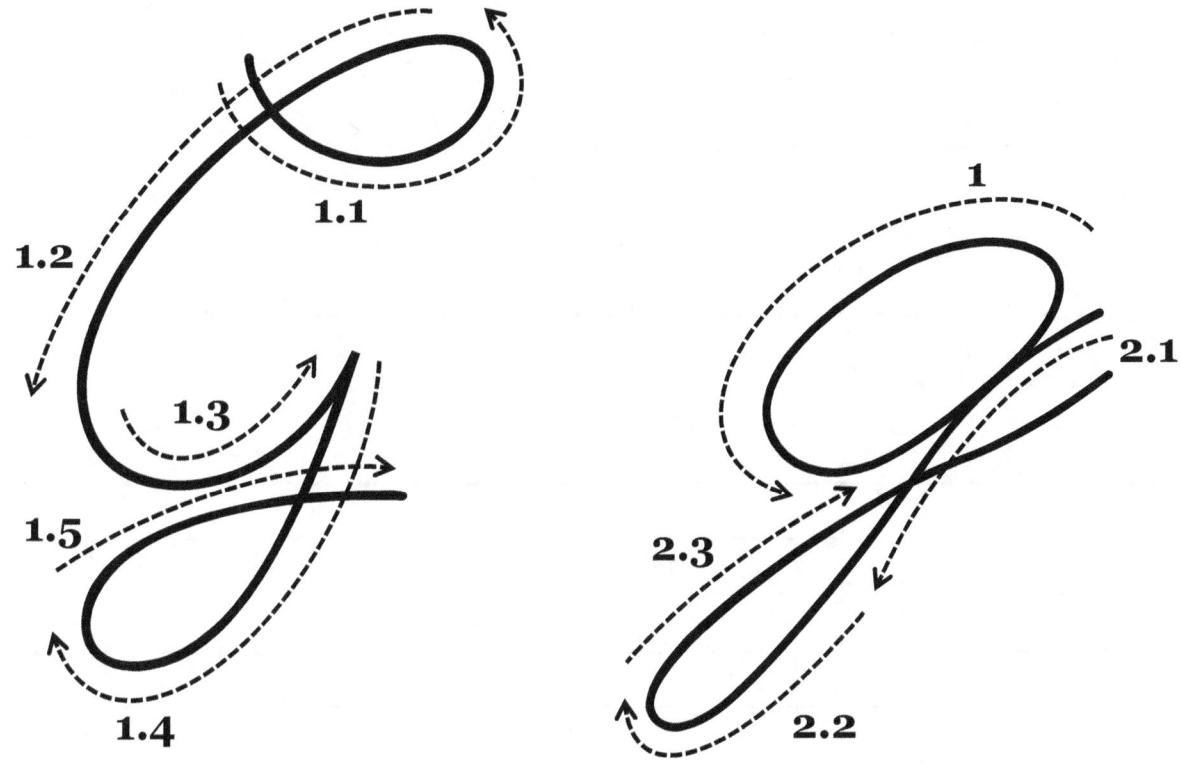

G G G G G G G G G

$\mathcal{G}$ $\mathcal{G}$ $\mathcal{G}$ $\mathcal{G}$ $\mathcal{G}$ $\mathcal{G}$ $\mathcal{G}$ $\mathcal{G}$ $\mathcal{G}$

$\mathcal{G}$ $\mathcal{G}$ $\mathcal{G}$

$\mathcal{G}$

$\mathcal{G}$

$\mathcal{G}$

$\mathcal{G}$

$\mathcal{G}$

$\mathcal{G}$

$\mathcal{G}$

$\mathcal{G}$

<u>Letter H</u>

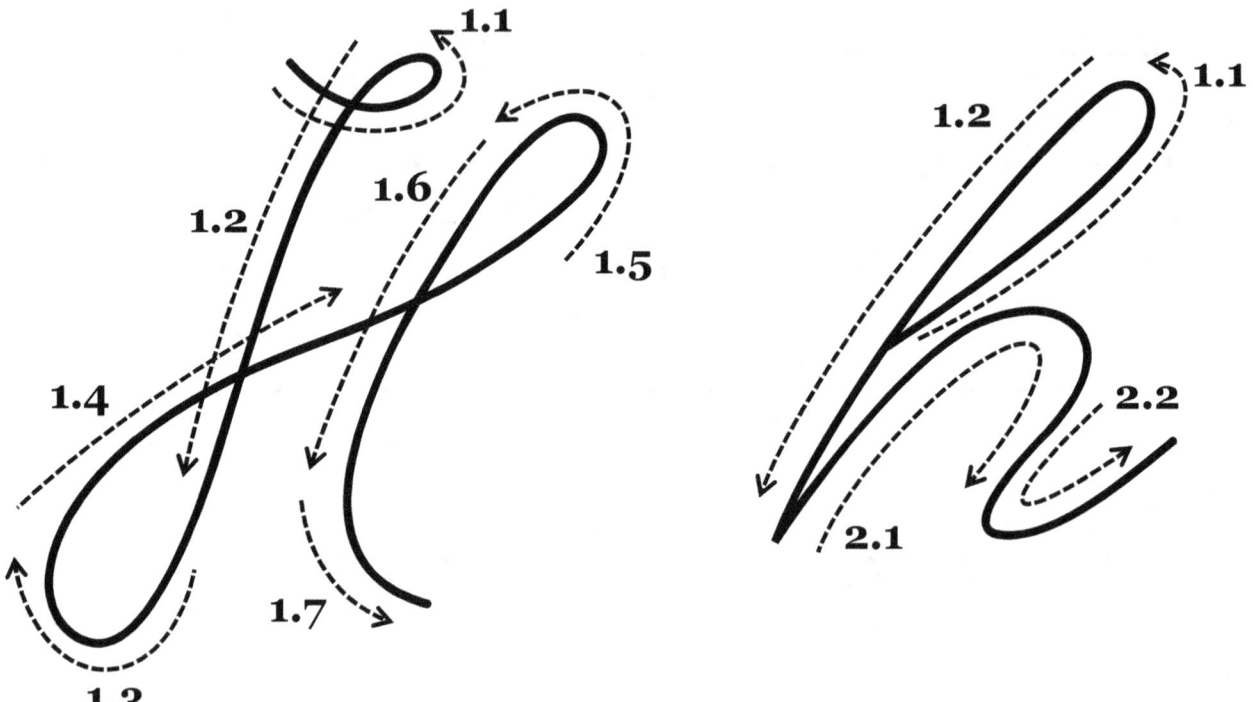

h h h h h h h h

h h h

h

h

h

h

h

h

h

Letter I

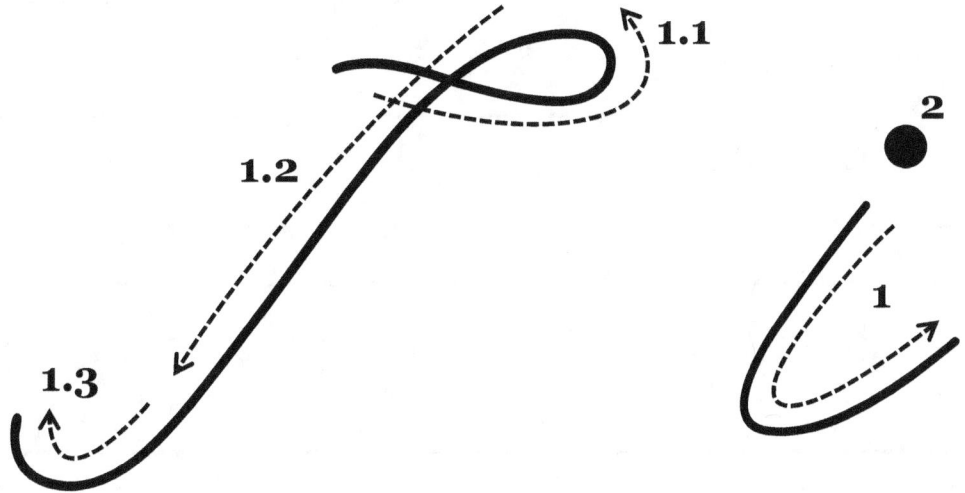

1.1

1.2

1.3

1

2

i *i*

Letter J

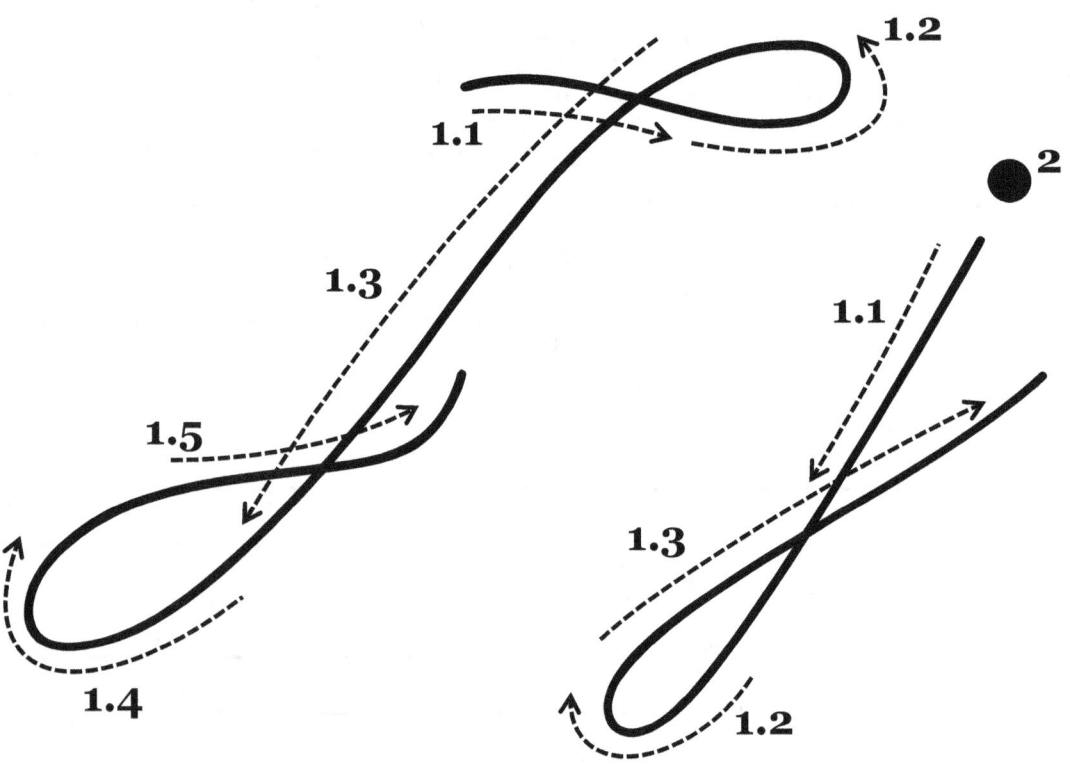

_j_ _j_

Letter K

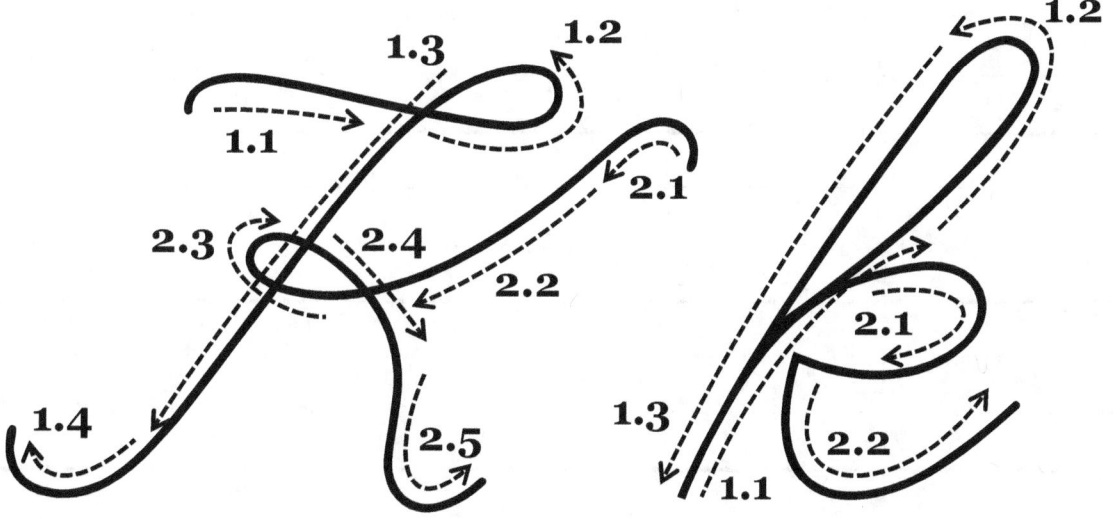

𝒦 𝒦 𝒦 𝒦 𝒦 𝒦 𝒦 𝒦

k k k k k k k k

k k k

k

k

k

k

k

k

k

k

Letter L

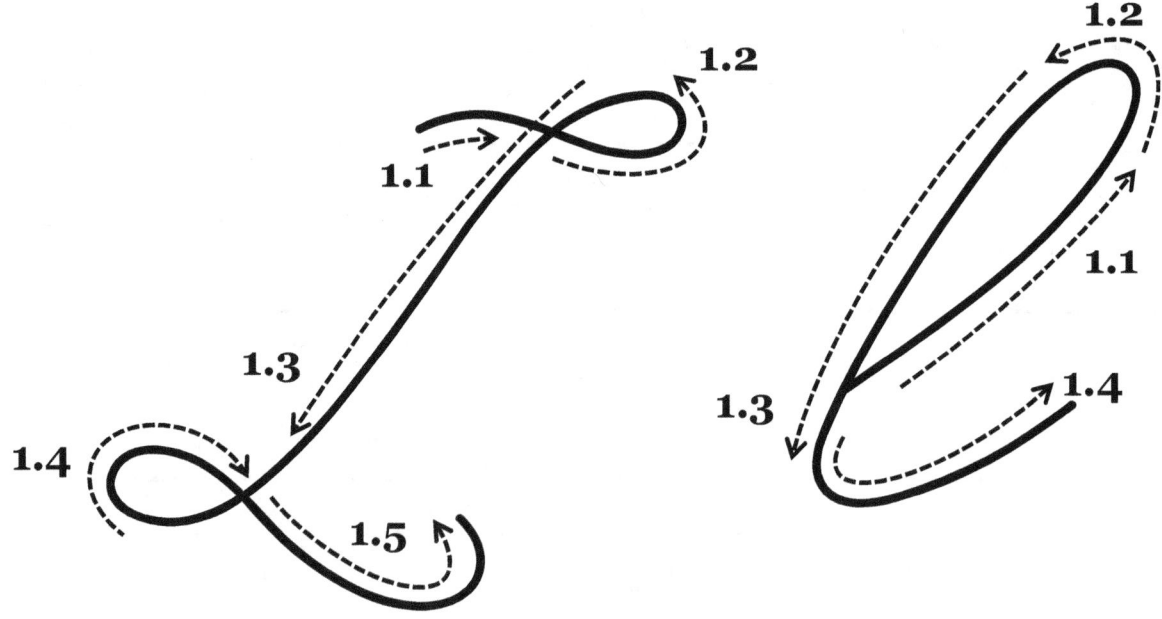

ℓ ℓ ℓ ℓ ℓ ℓ ℓ ℓ ℓ ℓ

ℓ ℓ ℓ

ℓ

ℓ

ℓ

ℓ

ℓ

ℓ

ℓ

Letter M

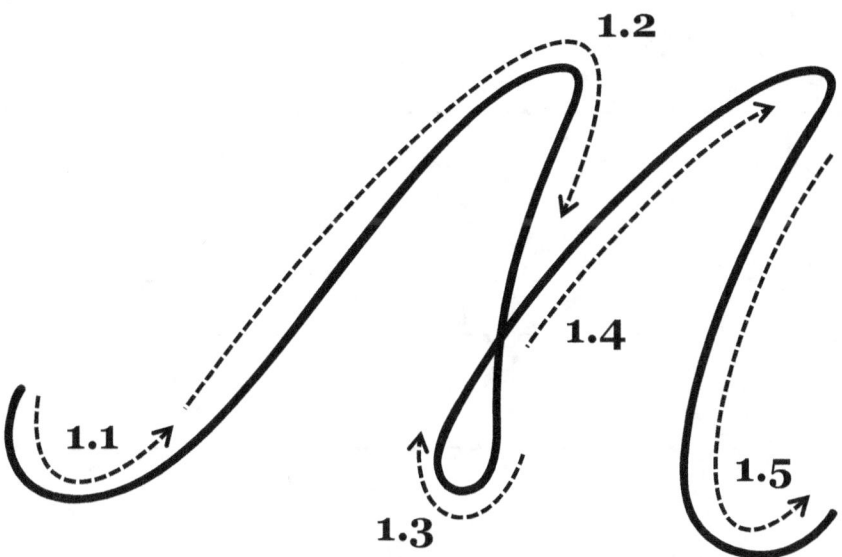

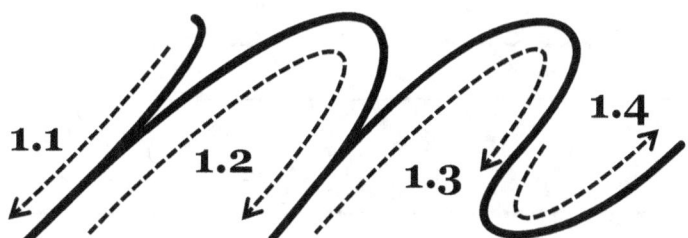

M M M M M M

m m m m m m m

m m m

m

m

m

m

m

m

m

m

Letter N

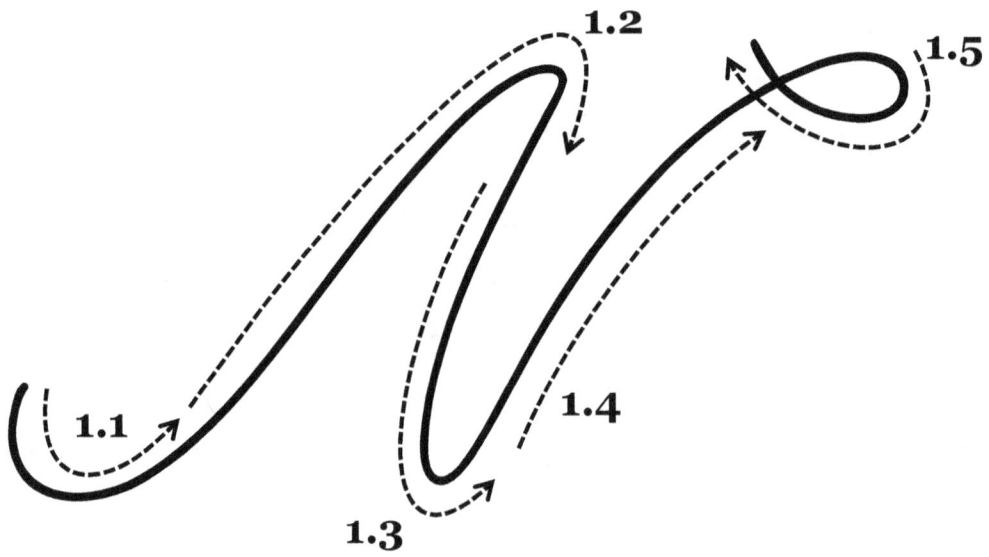

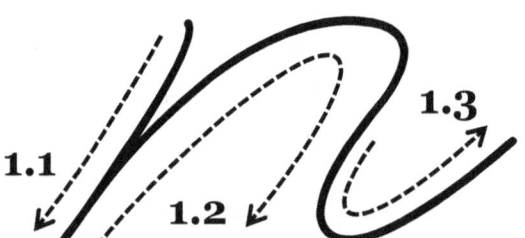

n n n n n n n n n n

n n n n

n

n

n

n

n

n

n

n

Letter O

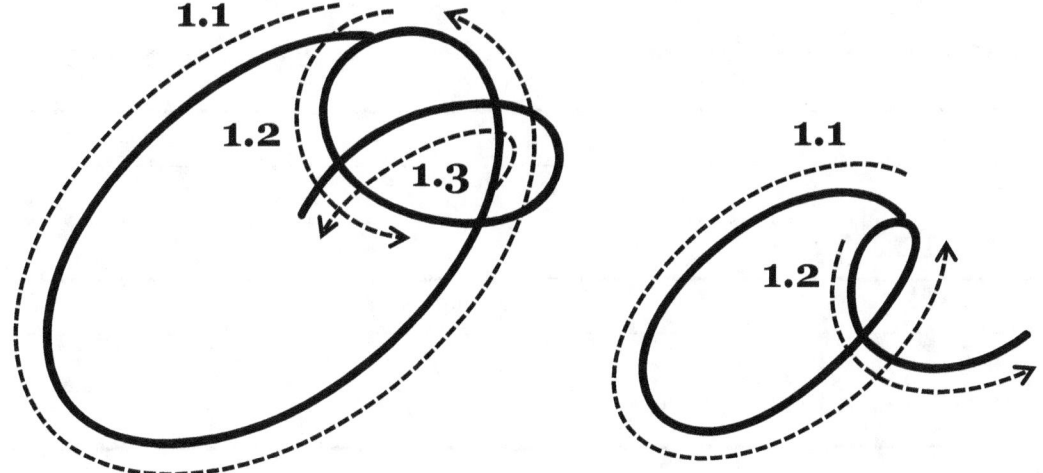

𝒶 𝒶 𝒶 𝒶 𝒶 𝒶 𝒶 𝒶 𝒶 𝒶 𝒶

𝒶 𝒶 𝒶

𝒶

𝒶

𝒶

𝒶

𝒶

𝒶

𝒶

𝒶

Letter P

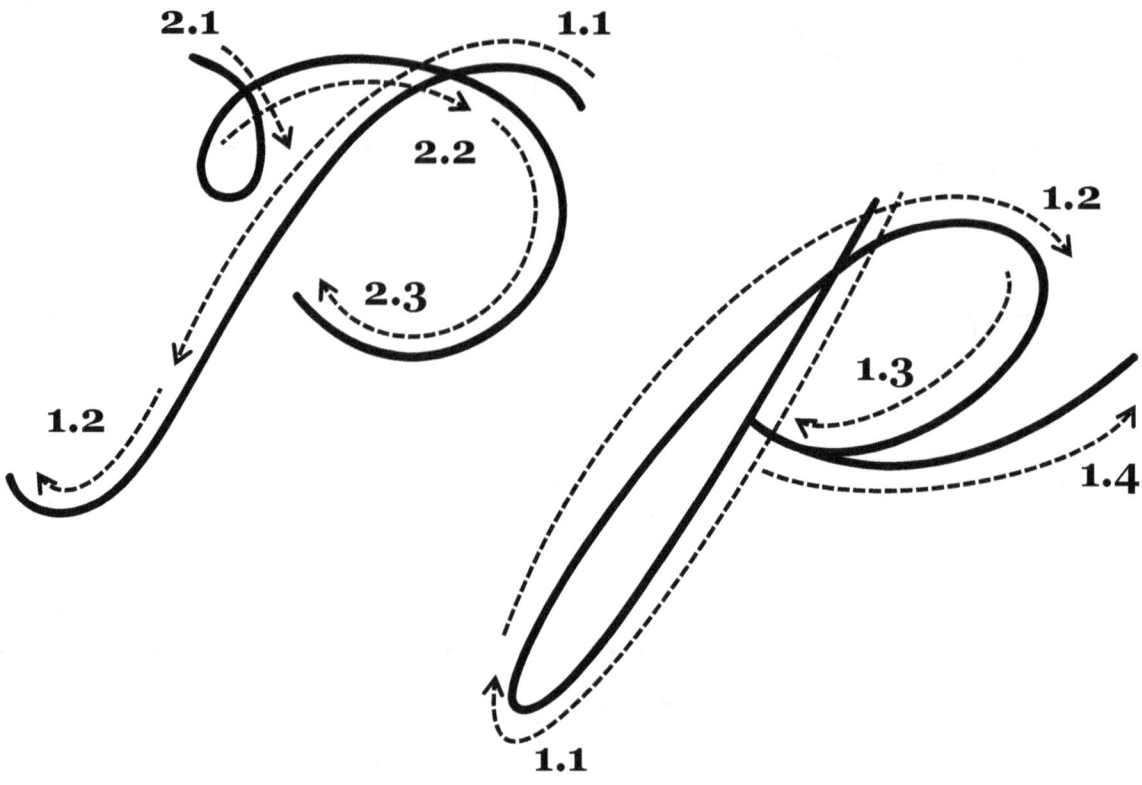

Letter Q

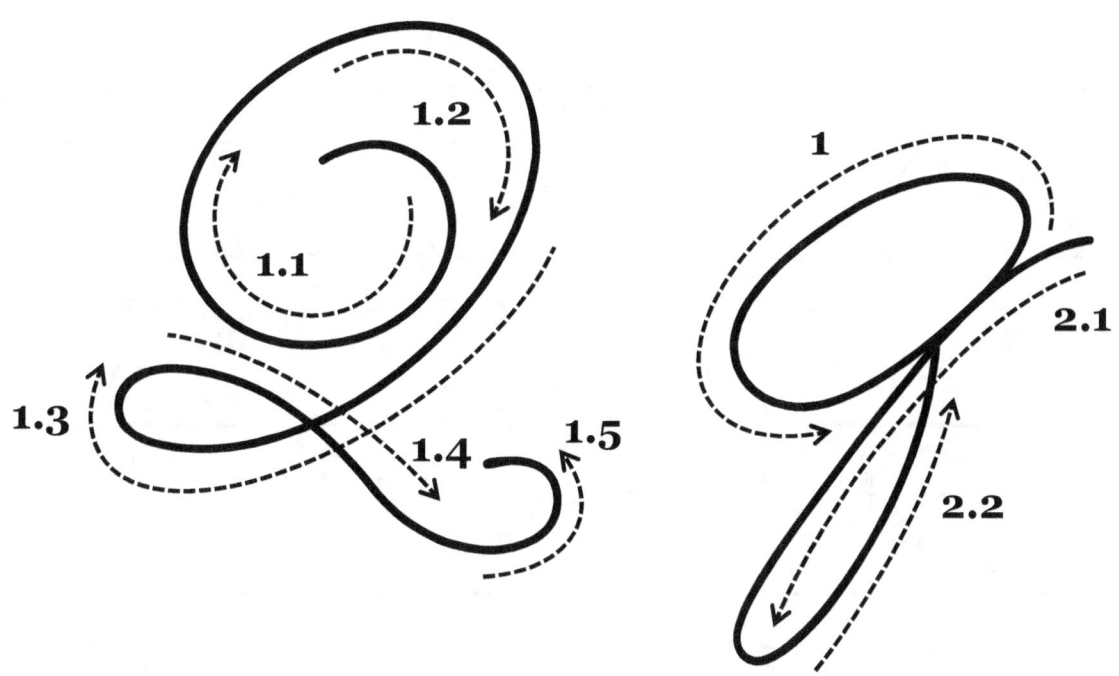

g g g g g g g g g g g

g g g

g

g

g

g

g

g

g

Letter R

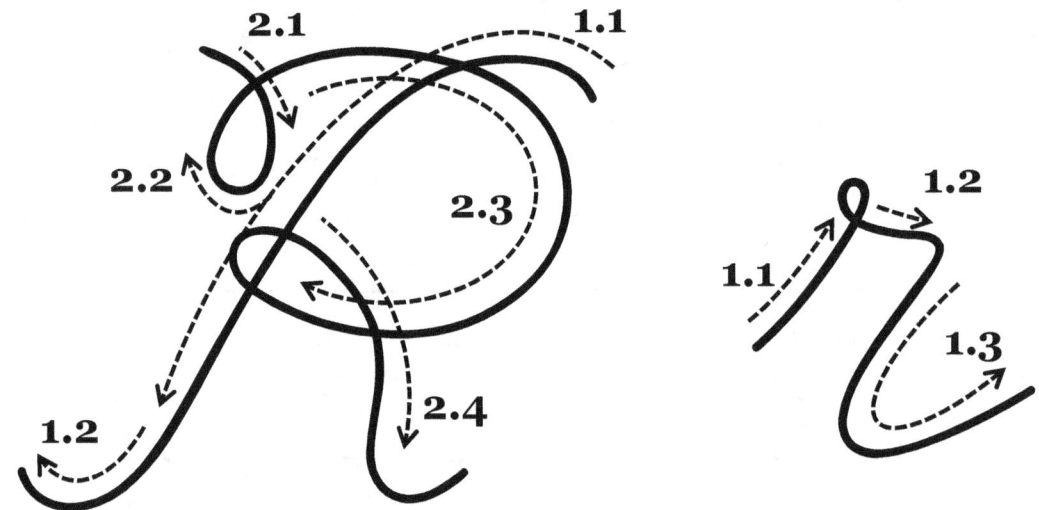

$\mathcal{R}$ $\mathcal{R}$

Letter S

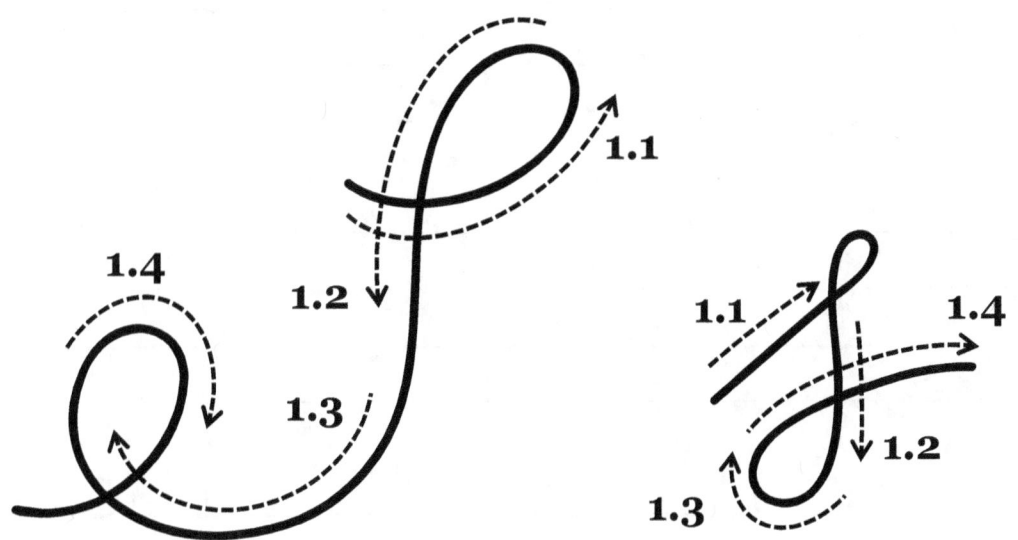

Letter T

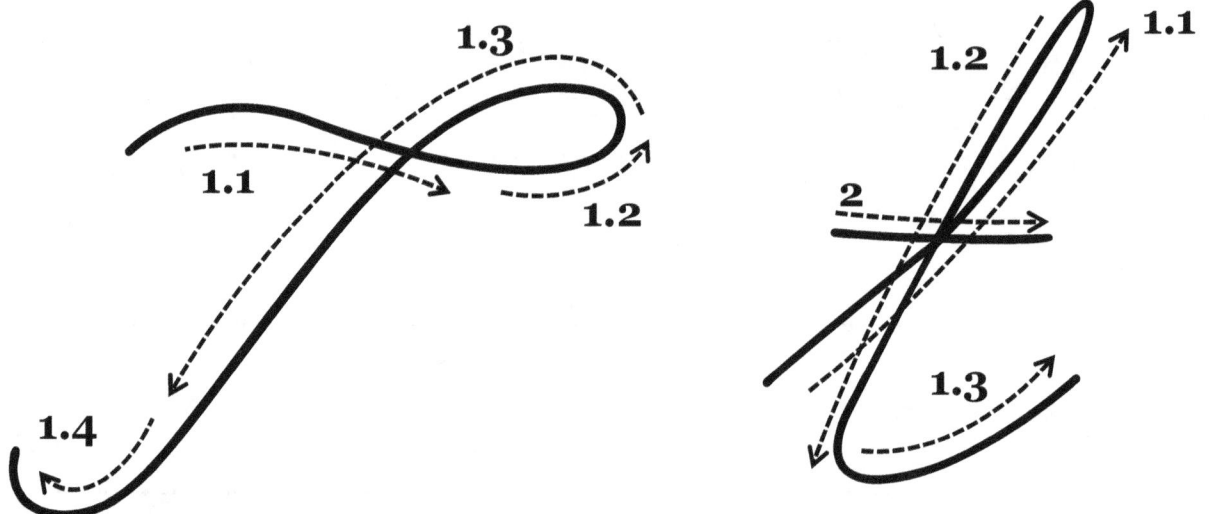

Letter U

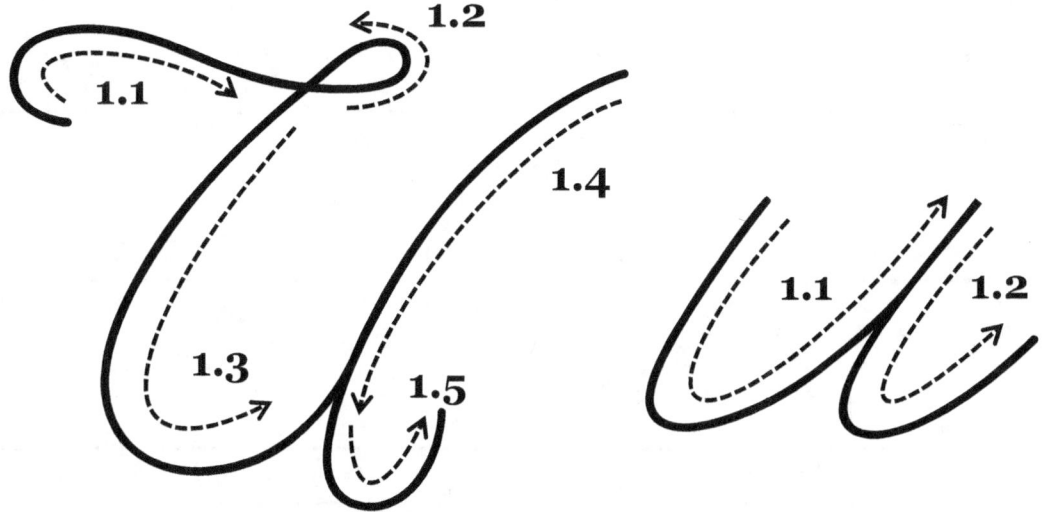

$\mathcal{U}\ \mathcal{U}\ \mathcal{U}\ \mathcal{U}\ \mathcal{U}\ \mathcal{U}\ \mathcal{U}$

U U 𝒰 𝒰 𝒰 𝒰 𝒰 𝒰 𝒰

𝒰 𝒰 𝒰

𝒰

𝒰

𝒰

𝒰

𝒰

𝒰

𝒰

𝒰

Letter V

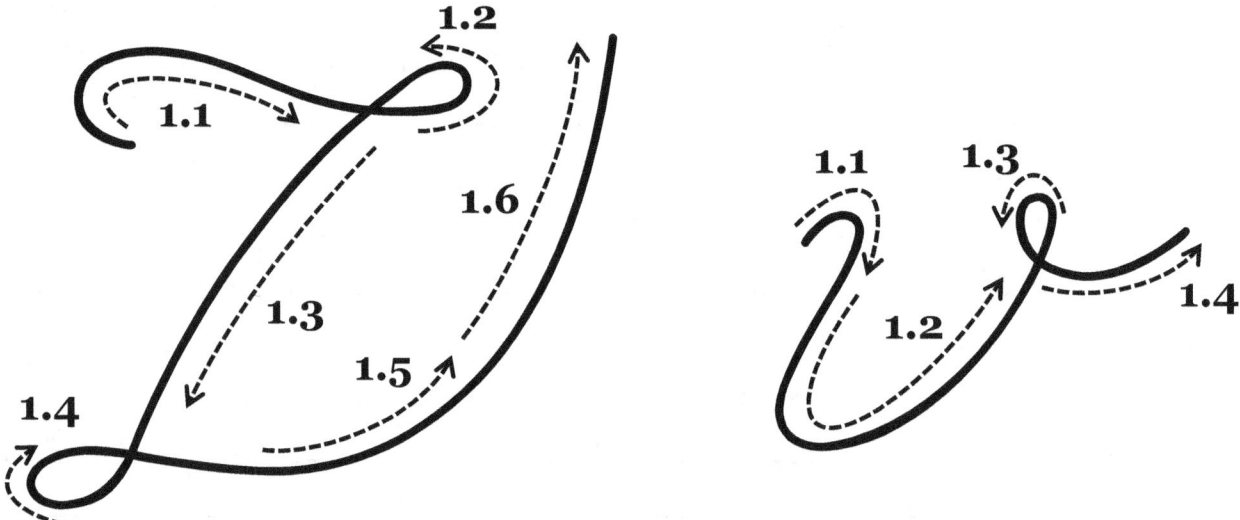

v v v v v v v v v

v v v

v

v

v

v

v

v

v

v

Letter W

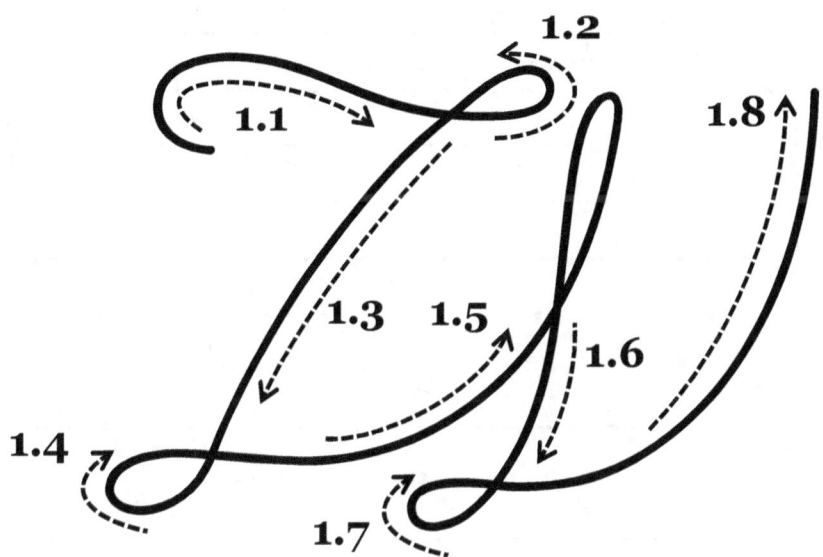

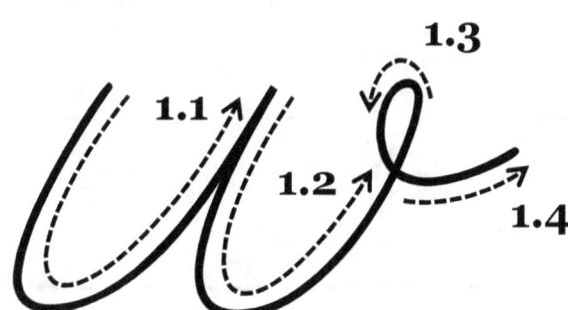

𝒲 𝒲 𝒲 𝒲 𝒲 𝒲 𝒲 𝒲

Letter X

X X x x x x x x x x

x x x

x

x

x

x

x

x

x

x

Letter Y

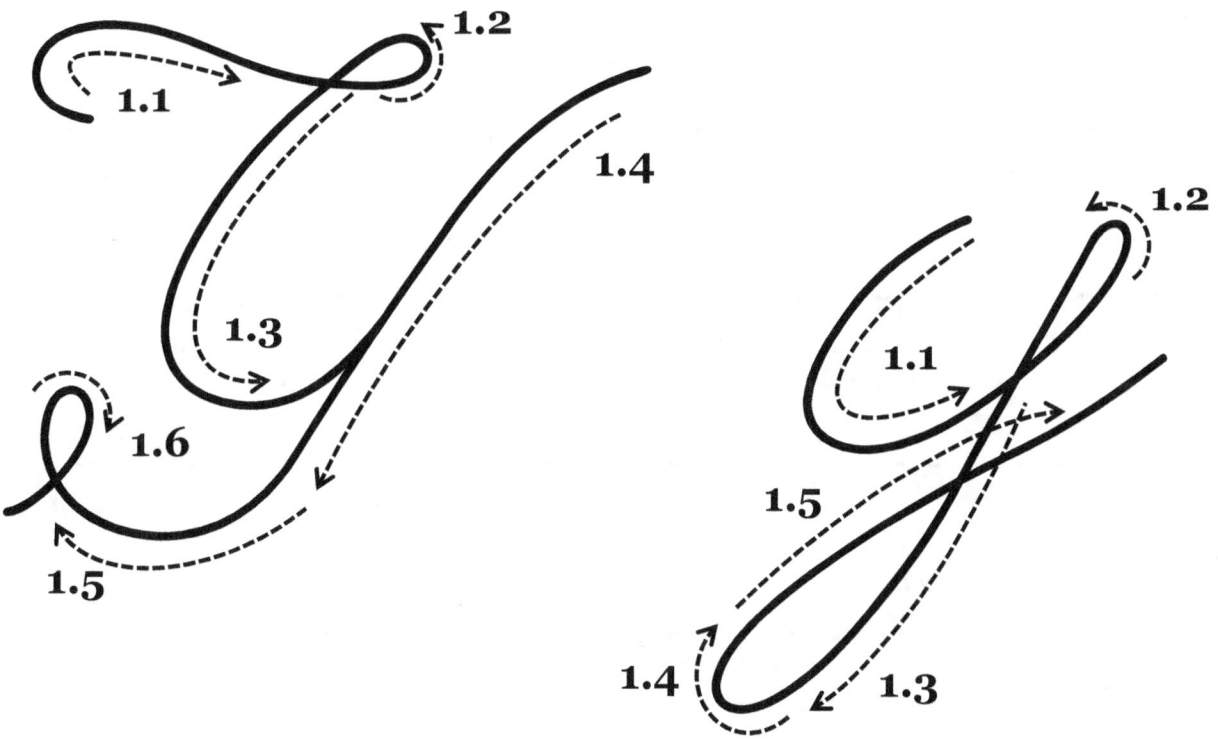

Letter Z

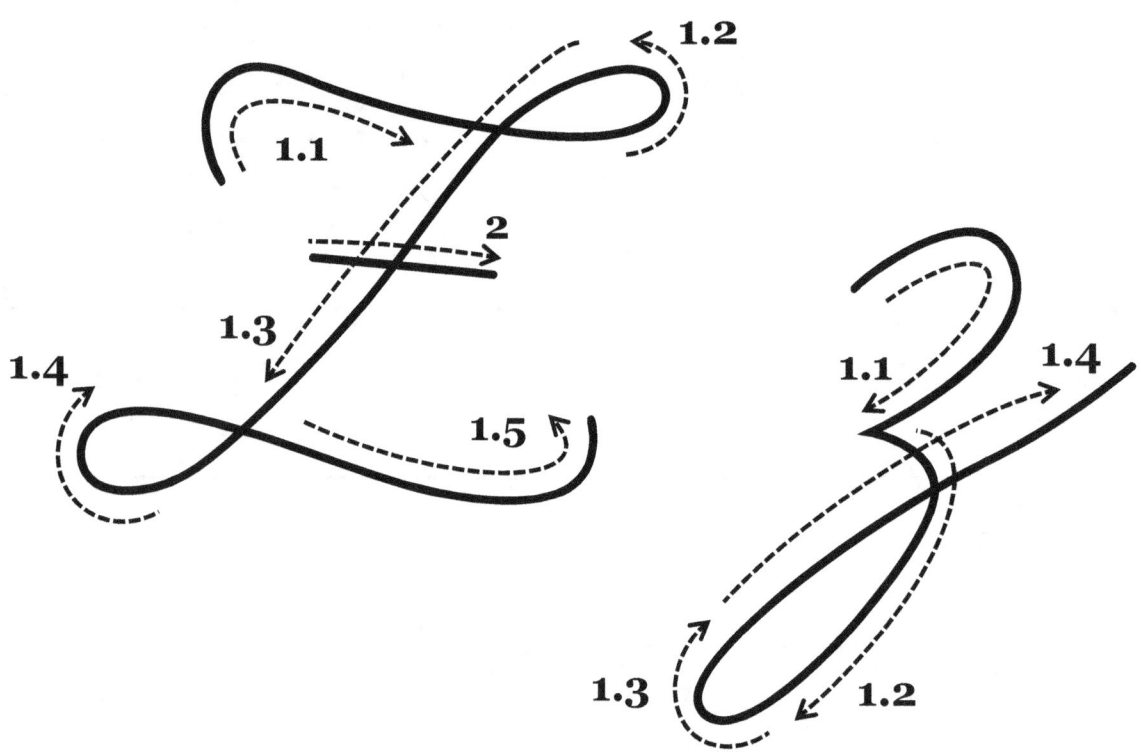

Z Z

Z Z

Part II

The second part of the book contains full words starting with each letter of the alphabet. All words are written in the same modern script font as before.

apple *apple*

ant *ant*

admire *admire*

actor *actor*

Amelia *Amelia*

bee *bee*

bright *bright*

ball *ball*

baby *baby*

Bella *Bella*

cat cat

corn corn

cute cute

car car

Carol Carol

dance dance

doll doll

day day

dog dog

David David

ear *ear*

eat *eat*

enter *enter*

eager *eager*

Europe *Europe*

fall *fall*

flower *flower*

fit *fit*

fur *fur*

France *France*

glow *glow*

green *green*

grace *grace*

goose *goose*

Greece *Greece*

house *house*

hill *hill*

hop *hop*

hat *hat*

Hungary *Hungary*

idea *idea*

inside *inside*

ice *ice*

inner *inner*

Italy *Italy*

joy *joy*

jelly *jelly*

jet *jet*

jar *jar*

July *July*

keep *keep*

koala *koala*

kitten *kitten*

kite *kite*

Kailey *Kailey*

lion *lion*

left *left*

little *little*

love *love*

London *London*

mint *mint*

minute *minute*

mercy *mercy*

move *move*

Madrid *Madrid*

null *null*

nice *nice*

new *new*

never *never*

Norway *Norway*

open

orange

origin

oasis

Oakland

pet pet

pine pine

pink pink

paw paw

Paris Paris

105

quill *quill*

quite *quite*

quick *quick*

quake *quake*

Queens *Queens*

ride *ride*

rest *rest*

rich *rich*

ripe *ripe*

Rome *Rome*

see see

squid squid

snow snow

slope slope

Spain Spain

tiny tiny

tooth tooth

tickle tickle

tree tree

Texas Texas

upper upper

united united

unity unity

untold untold

Ukraine Ukraine

vault *vault*

valve *valve*

vouch *vouch*

very *very*

Venice *Venice*

win win

wonder wonder

wall wall

wrist wrist

Wade Wade

xylem

xenon

xenopus

xyster

Xander

young *young*

year *year*

yield *yield*

you *you*

Yemen *Yemen*

zebra *zebra*

zoo *zoo*

zinc *zinc*

zipper *zipper*

Zeke *Zeke*